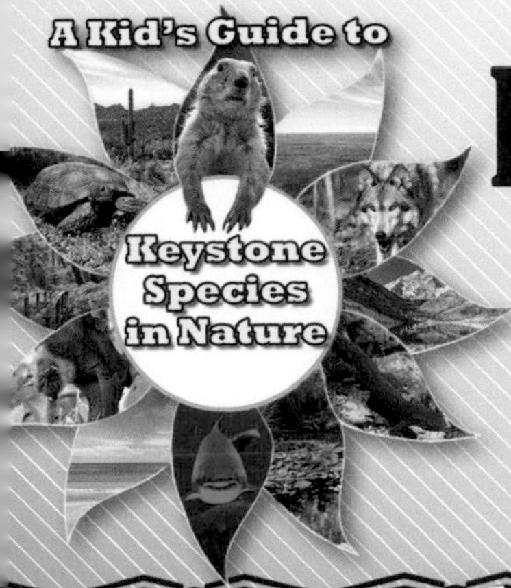

A Kid's Guide to

Keystone Species in Nature

Keystone Species that Live in Grasslands

BONNIE HINMAN

Mitchell Lane
PUBLISHERS
P.O. Box 196
Hockessin, DE 19707
www.mitchelllane.com

Mitchell Lane

PUBLISHERS

Printing   1   2   3   4   5   6   7   8

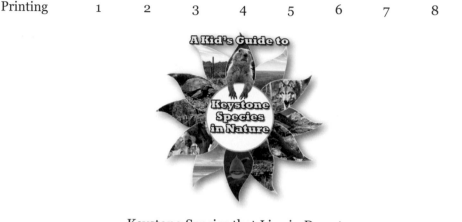

Keystone Species that Live in Deserts
Keystone Species that Live in Forests
Keystone Species that Live in Grasslands
Keystone Species that Live in the Mountains
Keystone Species that Live in Ponds, Streams, and Wetlands
Keystone Species that Live in the Sea and Along the Coastline

Library of Congress Cataloging-in-Publication Data
Hinman, Bonnie.
 Keystone species that live in grasslands / by Bonnie Hinman.
    pages cm. — (A kid's guide to keystone species in nature)
 Includes bibliographical references and index.
 Audience: Ages 8 to 11.
 Audience: Grades 3 to 6.
 ISBN 978-1-68020-058-4 (library bound)
 1. Keystone species—Juvenile literature. 2. Grassland ecology—Juvenile literature. I. Title.
 QH541.15.K48H557 2015
 577.2'6—dc23
                                                              2015003176
 eBook ISBN: 978-1-68020-059-1

Contents

Words in **bold** throughout can be found in the Glossary.

Introduction

Most arches built today contain a single building block at the top that is the most important piece. This special piece can be found in the arches of soaring cathedrals, doorways in temples, and even simple buildings made out of wooden blocks. It is called a keystone, and it holds everything else together. Remove the keystone and the building or doorway is likely to collapse.

The same thing is true in nature. Certain species of animals and plants are so important to their **ecosystems**, that if they disappear, the whole system may collapse. They are called keystone species.

Some keystone species are large, like southern white rhinos, while others are quite small, like honey bees. But size doesn't matter in an ecosystem. All living things rely

A keystone of a palace archway

Wolves feast on a bison they killed.

on other species to survive. A keystone species plays an especially large role that affects many different species in an ecosystem. Some keystone species are at the top of a huge ecosystem like the Greater Yellowstone Ecosystem, while others may affect a tiny ecosystem in a river or forest. Whether the ecosystem is big or small, the result of a keystone species disappearing or being greatly reduced is the same. Just like one falling domino can cause many others to fall, the loss of a keystone species can lead to the extinction of many other species.

Today scientists are focusing more attention on preserving the natural balance in ecosystems. Identifying and protecting keystone species is an important part of their work.

Chapter 1

BLACK-TAILED PRAIRIE DOG

Did you know that prairie dogs aren't dogs at all? They belong to the squirrel family of mammals. They look like squirrels, but they have a larger body, bigger teeth, and a broader head. If you saw a prairie dog's head peeking out of a hole in the ground, you would think he was a squirrel, not a dog.

So why do we call them prairie dogs? Why don't we call them prairie squirrels? The answer is in the noises they make. They bark, they chitter, and they yip. Scientists say that a prairie dog makes twelve different noises.[1]

When explorers first crossed the Great Plains that stretch west from Kansas to the Rocky Mountains, they saw these small animals everywhere. They heard loud yipping and barking coming from the "dog towns." The animals lived in groups that sometimes covered many square miles of prairie.

French explorers gave the animals the name *petit chien* (puh-TEE she-YEHN) or "little dog," since the animals barked constantly. Later, Meriwether Lewis and William Clark of the famous Lewis and Clark Expedition called them prairie dogs.

Black-tailed prairie dogs often stand upright to watch for any signs of predators. If they spot trouble, they bark a loud warning to other prairie dogs and dive into their burrows.

There are five kinds of prairie dogs: black-tailed, Mexican, white-tailed, Gunnison's, and Utah prairie dogs. There are more black-tailed prairie dogs than any other type. They also have the largest **range** of all the prairie dogs.[2]

Family Life

Black-tailed prairie dogs live together in towns or colonies that may cover many acres. Their family unit is called a coterie (KOH-tuh-ree). The family usually has one or two males and three or four females. All of their young live in the coterie until they are about one to two years old. Young males will then move out to join another coterie. They may switch coteries many times in their lives. The females usually stay in the coterie where they were born. Often mothers, aunts, and sisters live in the same coterie.

The family lives in many groups of tunnels called burrows which are usually six to ten feet (two to three meters) below ground. Each burrow has as many as six entrances above ground. Burrows can be small with only a few rooms joined by tunnels. Other burrows, used by the same family for years, have many more rooms and as many as 108 feet (33 meters) of tunnels.

Sometimes prairie dog towns are subdivided into wards, which are made up of several coteries. This usually happens when the town is divided by an area that the prairie dogs can't burrow under, like a group of trees or a stream.

Even though the coteries are close together, the prairie dogs do not visit their neighbors. Each coterie has a territory on top of its burrows. The family fiercely defends this territory, which is about an acre in size. The grass or **forbs** in this area feed the members of the coterie.

Coteries do cooperate in one way. Prairie dogs are always on the lookout for predators. If a member of one coterie spots danger, he or she barks a warning to the

Prairie dog tunnels or burrows may have many rooms beneath the surface. There are sleeping rooms, food storage rooms, and rooms for mothers and their babies. The burrows protect prairie dogs from most large predators, but some smaller predators can fit inside the burrows. The endangered black-footed ferret crawls easily through prairie dog tunnels to find its favorite food—the black-tailed prairie dog.

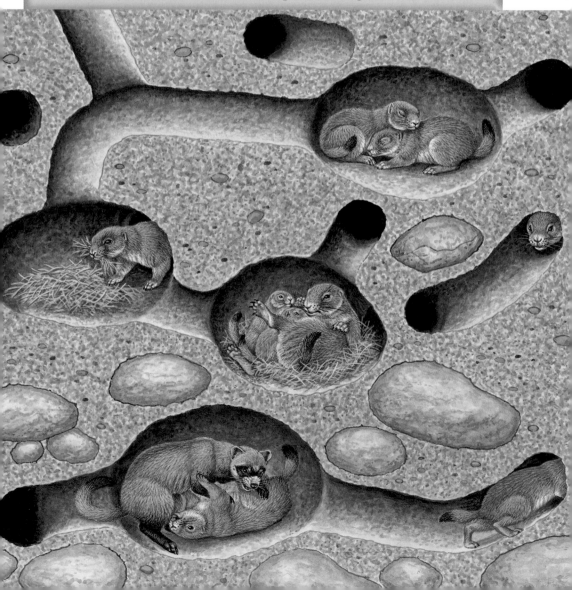

others. This sound gives all the residents of a prairie dog town time to dive underground to safety.

Black-tailed prairie dogs have one **litter** of pups a year. Most years a mother has three or four babies. They have no hair and their eyes are closed at birth. They will stay underground in a nursery room with their mother until they are about six weeks old. Then they poke their noses above ground for the first time.[3] They are fully grown at about eight months.

Black-tailed prairie dogs eat many kinds of grasses and forbs and a few insects like grasshoppers. Eating the grass around their burrows serves two purposes. It provides them with food and it also keeps the grass low so the prairie dogs can see predators. A prairie dog on lookout duty stands on the rim or top of the mound surrounding his burrow. With the grass cut close to the ground, he can see long distances.[4]

Trouble for Prairie Dogs

This lawn mowing habit has caused lots of trouble for black-tailed prairie dogs in the last hundred years. Before the Great Plains had settlers, there were millions of prairie dogs living everywhere. But when farmers and ranchers arrived, they wanted to get rid of prairie dog towns.

The settlers believed that the prairie dogs ate the grass that cows needed. They also thought that their cows would break their legs falling in the burrows. The farmers and ranchers did everything they could to get rid of the prairie dogs. Prairie dogs have been shot, trapped, poisoned, and drowned.

Research shows that in some areas prairie dogs do eat farmers' crops. However, scientists have also shown that cows prefer to eat the grass in and near prairie dog towns. When the grass is cut by the prairie dogs, it grows back quickly. Prairie dogs disturb the soil in a way that mixes it, and also allows it to absorb more water. This helps the grasses and other plants grow faster. Prairie dogs leave their waste above ground, which is filled with nutrients that are absorbed by the soil. The plants growing in this soil are in turn more nutritious for the animals that eat them.[5] Cows that eat grass where the prairie dogs live may be healthier. Scientists have also learned that cows rarely break their legs in prairie dog burrows. They know to step around the holes.[6]

The argument continues today. Black-tailed prairie dogs have lost about 95 percent of their population as a result of all the efforts to get rid of them. There are ranchers and farmers who want to save prairie dogs, though. In some areas black-tailed prairie dog populations are holding their own or even growing.

Giving Food and Shelter on the Prairies

Because many other species depend on black-tailed prairie dogs for survival, they are a keystone species. Coyotes, badgers, prairie falcons, golden eagles, hawks, and rattlesnakes all eat prairie dogs. The prairie dog is the main food source for the black-footed ferret, one of the most endangered mammals in the United States. Saving the prairie dog could also save the black-footed ferret.

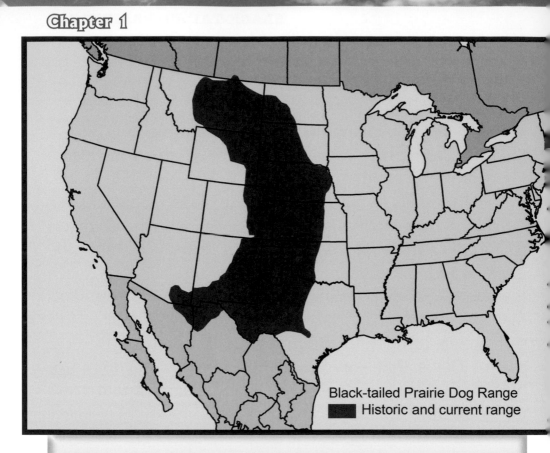

Black-tailed Prairie Dog Range
Historic and current range

Hundreds of millions of black-tailed prairie dogs once lived in the shaded area on the map above. Some scientists believe there were more of them than any other mammal in North America. Today they only occupy about 2 to 3 percent of the land in their original range, with an estimated 5 percent of their original population remaining.

Black-tailed prairie dogs don't only provide food for other species, they provide homes for them as well. Burrowing owls and cottontail rabbits live in empty burrows along with toads, salamanders, and black widow spiders.

Prairie dogs are vital to the food chain in the grasslands where they live. Without prairie dogs, many other species would leave or even become extinct. Life would be forever changed on the prairies.

Lewis and Clark and the Petit Chiens

Meriwether Lewis and William Clark set out from St. Louis, Missouri, in May 1804 to travel west to the Pacific Ocean. This journey was the Lewis and Clark Expedition. Lewis and Clark recorded 122 new animals and 178 new plants.[7]

By September, they had reached Nebraska, where William Clark carefully described the prairie dog. He wrote in his journal that the French explorers had been right to name the animals petit chiens, or small dogs, because in some ways that's what they looked like. The explorers poured water in a burrow to capture a prairie dog alive. They killed another one and ate it for supper.

The following spring Lewis and Clark shipped several plants and animals back to President Thomas Jefferson. It is not known if the prairie dog they sent was the same one they had caught the previous fall. The shipment's journey by boat to Washington, DC, covered 4,000 miles (6,400 kilometers) and took four months. The prairie dog arrived alive and was sent to a natural history museum in Philadelphia.[8]

FORT CLATSOP
BLACKFEET
COLUMBIA RIVER
NEZ PERCE
SHOSHONE
GREAT FALLS
THREE FORKS
SNAKE RIVER
FORT MANDAN
boundary not determined
SIOUX
Nebraska
PITTSBURGH •
• PHILADELPHIA
• WASHINGTON D.C.
SPANISH TERRITORY
LOUISIANA
ACQUIRED BY THE US IN 1803
SAINT CHARLES
CAMP WOOD
ST. LOUIS
UNITED STATES

LEWIS AND CLARK EXPEDITION 1804–1806

Chapter 2

BISON

Is a bison a buffalo? Aren't buffalo those big shaggy animals that look like they have a muff around their necks? Or are these fast-running bundles of fur really bison? That is a good question to ask.

The answer is that there are no true buffalo in North America. There is a water buffalo in Asia and an African buffalo in Africa. They are only distantly related to the bison that live in North America.[1]

Maybe the first American settlers called the animals buffalo because they looked like the water and African buffalo. Sometimes settlers called them the French for oxen, *les boeufs* (ley beuhf). Perhaps this word changed to buffalo. Whatever the reason, people have called bison "buffalo" since the first American settlers arrived.[2]

Scientists estimate that twenty to thirty million bison lived in North America before settlers arrived.[3] They lived from Canada to Mexico and from the Rocky Mountains to the Appalachian Mountains. By 1889 there were only a little more than a thousand bison left in North America.[4]

The new settlers turned out to be the worst enemies of bison. Native Americans had always hunted bison for food, clothing, and shelter. They killed what was needed

Bison are megaherbivores (MEG-uh-hur-buh-vawrs). Although they only eat plants, they can grow to 2,000 pounds (900 kilograms). Only a few other species of megaherbivores still live today, including elephants, rhinos, and hippos. Before the end of the last Ice Age (about ten thousand years ago) however, now-extinct megaherbivores like mastodons and woolly mammoths were common on Earth.

and no more. As east coast settlers moved west to claim new land, they killed the bison, too. However, they killed many more than they needed.

Hunters bragged about how many bison they killed in a day. Many killed only for the hides, and left the rest of the animal to rot in the grass. While some bison meat was shipped east for restaurants, it wasn't easy to keep fresh since refrigerated train cars had not yet been invented.

Daily Life for Bison

Bison are herbivores (HUR-buh-vawrs), meaning that they eat only plants. A full-grown male bison can weigh 2,000 pounds (900 kilograms), while a full-grown female can weigh as much as 1,000 pounds (450 kilograms). Males and females are between 6 and 6.5 feet (1.8 to 2 meters) tall at the shoulder and 10 to 12.5 feet (3 to 3.8 meters) long.[5] It takes a lot of plants to feed an animal of this size.

Bison eat on the move. They are roamers and have no special territories. They go where the good grass and other plants grow. Sometimes they stop to chew their cud just as cows do. This means that the grass in a bison's stomach gets moved back to his or her mouth to be chewed again. This method is how they digest their food and get the most nutrition from it.

Bison like grass more than any other food. They will eat many different kinds, like blue stem, buffalo, and gama grass. They also eat some other plants. But grass is a bison's favorite dinner.

When they are fully grown, male bison are called bulls and female bison are called cows. Bulls and cows live in separate herds most of the year. The cows keep all

This bison calf can count on Mom to take care of it for at least a year. The calf nurses for several months, but learns to eat grass at the same time. Bison calves are born in the spring. They need to grow big enough over the summer to survive the next winter.

of the calves with them. Only during mating season do the two herds live together. That's when the fights begin. Bulls fight each other to claim the cow they want as a mate. Most of the time it is more of an argument than an actual fight.

Bulls bellow loudly and constantly during mating season. They seem to say, "I'm here and I'm strong! Just try to push me around!" Bulls approach each other while stamping their feet. Then they may butt heads. Sometimes it leads to a real fight with horns swinging and blood gushing. Most of the time one of the bulls will back away, deciding that it is a good idea to let the other bull have this particular cow.[6]

Calves are born in the spring and stand and walk within minutes after birth. This ability gives them the most protection from predators like wolves or grizzly bears. They nurse their mother's milk at first and then begin to eat grass. They are almost fully grown by around four years old, but keep growing a little for three or four more years. Bison can live for fifteen to twenty-five years.

These two male bison are sizing each other up to see if they want to fight. There is probably a female bison nearby. Each of the males wants her for a mate. One of these two males will likely walk away without a fight. Fights take a lot of energy and could leave one or both bulls injured. It's probably easier to find another female.

Wallowing bison

Bison like to roll around on the ground at least a couple times a day, especially in the summer. They make shallow holes called wallows that have dust or mud in them. Scientists think bison like to be covered with dirt to get rid of biting insects and to help keep out the heat in the summer.[7] It probably also feels nice to get a good back scratching.

Saving the Bison

Early in the twentieth century some people began to realize that bison would soon be extinct if nobody helped them survive. The American Bison Society was founded in 1905 to help save the bison. The Society raised money to buy bison and move them to reserves where they could live. In twenty years there were thousands of bison living on the Midwestern plains. Today there are approximately five hundred thousand bison living in North America. Most of them live on ranches as livestock.[8]

Bison are an important part of American history, but they are also important to the prairies where they live. The wallows they create support other plants and animals. Since the dirt is tightly packed in these areas, grasses can't grow there. That means that other plants can grow without competing with the grasses for sunlight. The wallows also hold water when it rains, providing temporary homes to frogs, toads, and snakes.[9]

Bison improve the grasslands because of the way they eat grass. They graze in patches because they like certain

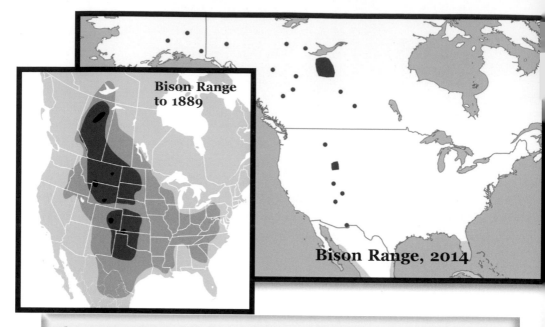

The maps above tell the sad story of the bison's disappearance. The light brown area of the map on the left shows where bison lived in North America before settlers arrived. The dark brown areas show where bison lived in 1870, and the black areas show their range as of 1889. The red areas on the map on the right show where bison lived in 2014.

grasses better than others. This patch grazing allows other plants to grow, and that in turn gives shelter and food to many small animals. In the areas that bison graze, for example, prairie dogs find more of the grasses and forbs they like.

Wolves and grizzly bears eat bison meat. Scavengers like buzzards and ravens depend on the dead carcasses of bison to provide food. They feast on the meat left behind by the wolves and grizzly bears.

It is exciting to see the huge wooly animals in parks and reserves. But they are also important in their ecosystem. That is why scientists, ranchers, and others continue their work to bring bison back to the grasslands.

Buffalo Chips

The Plains Indians hunted bison to use for food, containers, clothing, tools, boots, and many other things. Pioneers discovered, as the Native Americans had, that dried bison **dung** made good fuel for fires.

The round piles of dried poop were called buffalo chips. The open plains had few trees to use for fuel. Buffalo chips burned with a nice hot fire and did not smell bad. The best part was that buffalo chips were everywhere just waiting to be picked up.

The millions of bison that roamed the plains left plenty of fuel behind. The pioneers may not have liked burning poop at first, but they changed their minds when the fires kept them warm and helped them cook supper.

Chapter 3

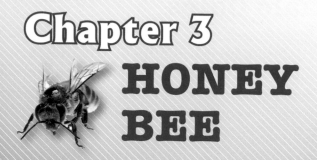

HONEY BEE

Sweet sticky honey—it tastes so good. We love that bees give us such a treat to put on toast or biscuits or pancakes. While honey is tasty, making it is not the most important thing that bees do.

Bees pollinate many kinds of plants. Pollination is like starting a plant's engine. After it happens, the plant produces fruit, berries, vegetables, nuts, or seeds. Imagine how boring our meals would be if we couldn't have apple pie, almonds, mustard, guacamole, orange juice, or strawberry shortcake again.

The pollination process is simple enough, but it takes some complicated work to get the job done. Pollen from the male part of a flower has to reach the stigma or female part of another flower. The wind can do this for some plants. Many more need some extra help to physically move the pollen to the **ovules**. Sometimes hummingbirds do this physical work. Many kinds of insects including wasps work as pollinators, too. But bees spend much more of their lives collecting pollen than other insects do.[1]

Bees aren't the only pollinators but they do more than their share of the work pollinating plants. There are

A worker honey bee may travel several miles away from the hive to collect pollen. This bee will visit between fifty and one hundred flowers on each trip before she returns to the hive. In her lifetime a worker bee will produce about one-twelfth of a teaspoon of honey.

thousands of species of bees. The most common ones are bumble bees, carpenter bees, sweat bees, and honey bees. All are important to their habitat, but honey bees do a lot of the pollinating for farmers' crops.

Honey bees are a keystone species in their natural homes of Africa, Europe, and Asia. Today they are a keystone species in North and South America, too. **Immigrants** from Europe brought them to America because the new settlers understood how important honey bees are. They wanted honey bees to pollinate the trees in their orchards and the plants in their fields. Native bees could pollinate these plants, also, but they couldn't be controlled like the European honey bees. Whenever farmers needed bees to pollinate their crops, they could bring in honey bees to do the work.

A Bee's Life

Honey bees can live in hollow trees or barn rafters or any other place where they can get together. However, they live mostly in man-made hives. Hives can be different shapes but today they are usually large square boxes that sit in a field or orchard. Inside, the bees build honeycombs—small connected cells of wax. These cells provide places for honey bees to live, store food, and raise baby bees.

Beekeepers are the men or women who take care of the hives. Bees do not need help to do their work, but they do need protection sometimes. The beekeeper keeps an eye on the bees to make sure they are healthy and have food for the winter.

A beekeeper is a honey bee's best friend. The keeper checks the hive many times a year to be sure that the bees have enough food. He or she also checks for diseases. Some experienced beekeepers handle bees without gloves, but beginners should not leave their gloves at home.

The Bees in a Beehive

Three kinds of bees live in a beehive: queen bees, drone bees, and worker bees. Queen bees lay the eggs for the next generation of bees. There's usually only one queen bee in each hive.

Drone bees are the males. Drones do not seem to have any duty in the hive other than to mate with the queen. Once mating is done, they die. There can be up to a few thousand drones in a hive at any one time.

Worker bees are the ones buzzing from flower to flower in a field or garden. They are females, but do not mate and lay eggs. Their name describes what they do. A worker bee performs all of the tasks needed to maintain a beehive. There can be tens of thousands of worker bees in a hive.

All worker bees have a specific role to play in their hives. Which role depends on the age of the bee. When a young worker bee emerges from her wax cell after **pupating**, her first job is that of cleaning up the hive. Then she feeds the developing **larvae**. Next the new worker bee helps tend to the queen.

When a worker bee is about twelve days old, she begins to produce the wax which is used to build the cells of the honeycomb. She also works at changing nectar into honey using special chemicals in her body. Later, she stands guard at the entrance of the hive, making sure that only bees that are part of the family can get in.

At about two to three weeks old, worker bees leave the hive to become **foragers**. They look high and low for nectar and pollen sources. They bring the pollen and nectar back to the hive for other worker bees to process into honey. This is the most dangerous part of a worker bee's life.

There are predators like wasps among the flowers and sometimes there may be **pesticides** on the plants. Weather can be hard on worker bees, too. Many scientists think that worker bees wear themselves out. They live for several weeks to months while a queen might live for several years.

Worker bees called scout bees look for flowers that have nectar and pollen. Sometimes the nectar's sweet smell attracts the bees, and sometimes a flower's color draws them in. Once the scout bee finds an area with lots of food, she returns to the hive to tell the foragers where it is.

The foragers follow directions and get to work. Each bee finds a good flower and burrows into the middle of the bloom. She sucks up the nectar with her tongue and stores it inside her body to carry home. The pollen from the flower's male parts sticks to her. She pushes most of this pollen into "pollen baskets" on her back legs. Then she buzzes off to the next flower.

pollen basket

pollen basket

From flower to flower the bee flies collecting nectar and pollen. Each time she visits a new flower, she leaves behind some of the pollen that she collected from another flower. This pollen falls onto the flower's female part, which later forms seeds.

The worker bee then returns to the hive to pass the nectar and pollen to another worker bee who will process the watery nectar into honey. Worker bees also make the pollen into bee bread, which is a high-protein food that the bees eat. The honey is stored for food to eat during the winter, when pollen becomes hard to find.

The seeds created in the flowers during pollination turn into fruits and vegetables like blueberries and pumpkins. But this important part of the worker bees' job is done by accident. They are only looking for food for themselves. But in the process, they feed a lot of people and animals, too!

Colony Collapse Disorder

In recent years honey bees have suffered from a disease called Colony Collapse Disorder (CCD). Bees suddenly leave their hives and don't return. From 2007 to 2013 in North America, more than ten million bee colonies were lost this way.[2] Scientists don't know yet what causes CCD. It's possible that there aren't enough wild plants remaining to feed the bees and keep them healthy. Diseases or pesticides could be harming the bees. Or it could be a combination of many causes.[3]

While scientists search for a solution to this problem, beekeepers do everything they can to help the bees survive. They can spot many diseases early and treat the colonies before they die out. The survival of honey bees is important to all of us. After all, if honey bees disappear, your favorite food might disappear, too.

Bees On the Loose

Honey bees have a behavior that can be alarming if it takes you by surprise. A large number of bees leave their hive and settle on a nearby tree limb or possibly on a fence post. With a loud buzzing sound, the bees settle into a big clump on the limb or other surface. This is called swarming.

Swarming is the natural way that bees start new colonies. Overcrowding is the main reason that beehives split. The old queen leaves the hive with more than half of the worker bees, and a new queen takes over the original hive.

The bees only fly a short distance at first because the queen can't fly far. They cluster around her to keep her safe while scout bees search for a new permanent home. When the scouts return to the swarm with news of a likely new home, the whole swarm flies off to make a new hive.

Chapter 4
SOUTHERN WHITE RHINOCEROS

The white rhino is not white at all. African white rhinos are gray. So why not call them gray rhinos? Scientists ask that question, too.

They may be called white because of a misunderstanding. Some people believe that Dutch-speakers called them *wijd* or "wide," but confused English-speakers thought that the word meant "white." Not all scientists think that this story is likely, however. No one can find any proof that the Dutch ever called a rhino "wijd." It's possible that the people who first described the rhinos thought they looked white because they had rolled in mud that later dried white. Nobody knows the answer for sure.[1]

Rhinos are the second-largest land animal in the world. Only elephants are bigger. There are five different species of rhinos, but only the white and black rhinos live in Africa. The Indian, Javan, and Sumatran rhinos live in Asia. Black rhinos are the same color as white rhinos: gray. White rhinos have a square upper lip so they can eat grass like a lawnmower. They put their heads to the ground and chomp away. Black rhinos have a hooked upper lip. They like to eat tree branches and shrubs and this lip helps them get a grip on the food.

Two southern white rhinos graze in Lake Nakuru National Park in Kenya. This park became a rhinoceros sanctuary in 1983. Hippos, giraffes, and hundreds of species of birds also live in the park.

There are two kinds of white rhinos in Africa. One is called the northern white rhino. This type is extinct in the wild. Only a few live in zoos in Europe and the United States, and in a park in Kenya. Scientists are trying to save the northern white rhino from total extinction, but it doesn't look good for them. The northern white rhinos that remain are getting older and may not ever have calves.[2]

Threats to the Southern White Rhino

The southern white rhino was also in trouble in the late 1800s. By 1900, less than one hundred were left. They have done much better than the northern type at increasing their numbers. There are at least twenty thousand southern white rhinos living in the wild now. They roam across the huge grasslands and **savannas** of Southern and Eastern Africa.[3]

Humans are the reason that rhinos have decreased in numbers. Adult rhinos are not normally attacked by natural predators. Sometimes the youngest rhinos are killed by lions, hyenas, or crocodiles. In the nineteenth and twentieth centuries, **trophy hunting** by man was the biggest threat. Today **poachers** kill rhinos for their horns. Rhino horns sell for a lot of money in many places in Asia.[4]

Buyers often use the horns to make a kind of medicine. There's not enough research to know for sure whether the horns can actually cure human diseases. But we do know that the horns can be cut without killing the rhinos. Just like our hair or fingernails, rhinos' horns grow back when cut. However, the poaching continues even as **conservation** groups and some governments try to stop it.

Southern White Rhino Basics

Southern white rhinos weigh from 3,000 to 8,000 pounds (1,400 to 3,600 kilograms) and are between 5 and 6 feet (1.5 to 1.8 meters) tall at the shoulder. They graze on grass at least half of the day. They have certain grasses that they prefer, so they move from patch to patch of that kind of grass. Rhinos also love to wallow in mud. This is their favorite thing to do on hot afternoons. It cools them and the mud coating also protects their skin from insects and sunburn.[5]

Female rhinos may have a calf once every two or three years. The **gestation** time for rhinos is about sixteen months. They have one calf at a time and the calves nurse for a few months before learning to eat grass. Rhino mothers are very protective of their calves. A calf may stay with his or her mother until the mother has her next baby. Even then the mothers and children often stay together in a group called a crash.

The adult male white rhino is called a bull and most of the time lives by himself. A bull doesn't reach breeding age until he is ten to twelve years old. Before that, he may live with other young bulls and sometimes with another adult female. Bulls have small territories that they mark with their urine and dung.

Females are called cows and are old enough to breed by six to seven years old. They have larger territories that may overlap several bulls' territories. Females do not defend their territories.

White rhinos live for up to fifty years. Most of the time rhinos are not aggressive toward each other or other animals or people. This is one of the reasons poachers have been able to kill so many of them.

Rhinos have excellent senses of hearing and smell, but their eyesight is poor. They can run up to twenty-five miles per hour (forty kilometers per hour) if provoked, but prefer to live at a slower pace. They communicate with each other with as many as eight sounds. They snort and snarl to say, "Stay away." A male squeals when he wants to stop a female from leaving his territory. A calf whines to show distress, usually to try to get Mom's attention.

Why Southern White Rhinos Are Important

The way that southern white rhinos graze the grasslands where they live has a big effect on the other plants and animals in the area. Studies show that grasslands where rhinos no longer graze have fewer plants for other animals to eat. Rhinos clip the grass in patches as they eat the particular kinds they like. These grasses are stronger than many other plants, so where there are no rhinos, the grasses take over the land. By eating the strongest grasses, the rhinos leave room for other plants and grasses to grow. Animals like antelope depend on these plants for food.[6]

Impala, zebra, and wildebeest also need the shorter grass that rhinos create. If the rhinos did not keep the grasslands grazed, grasses would grow too tall for these animals. Scientists have learned that when rhinos leave an area, the impala, zebra, and wildebeest leave too.[7]

Fossil records show that white rhinos have been around for as long as eight million years. This piece of living history could come to an end, however, if poachers are allowed to continue killing this invaluable keystone species.

All About Extinction

Any species can become extinct. This natural process has been happening since the days of the dinosaurs. A species is extinct when the last surviving member of that species dies. Although extinction is a natural process, it is happening these days at an alarming rate. Scientists say that if humans were not interfering and there were no major disasters, up to five species would naturally go extinct each year. In the twenty-first century scientists estimate that dozens of species go extinct every day.[8]

"Extinction" doesn't always mean a species is completely gone, however. When the only members left of a species live in zoos or other protected areas, they are extinct in the wild. Sometimes a species is **functionally** extinct because the members left will not be able to have babies. Perhaps they are too old or they are all male, or all female.

Currently, humans are the biggest cause of extinction. As we build our homes, schools, and stores, we destroy the grasses, forests, wetlands, and other habitats that many species live in. Sometimes people bring species to new lands where they have never been before. This new species might eat all the food that other species relied on. Although humans are part of the problem now, we can all become part of the solution. Learning about keystone species and sharing your knowledge with others is a great first step.

Poaching is one of the biggest threats to rhinos. Shown here is a skull of a rhino that was most likely killed for its horn.

Chapter 5

LEMMING

Lemmings are small furry rodents that live in the arctic or far northern parts of North America, Europe, and Asia. They became famous when they were shown in a 1958 documentary movie. Unfortunately, that documentary was very wrong.

The movie about these animals was called *White Wilderness*. Made by Walt Disney, *White Wilderness* showed the lives and behavior of several lemmings who lived in the far north. In the movie, a big group of lemmings ran at top speed only to leap over a cliff to their deaths. The narrator said they were committing **suicide**. Soon everyone believed that lemmings did this regularly. Books and later movies kept this belief alive.

When an area has too many lemmings, it becomes harder for them to find food. So many of them leave to find new homes, often running together in large groups. But they do not commit suicide. An investigation later revealed that the scene with the lemmings plunging to their deaths was staged. Lemmings don't even live in Alberta, Canada, where the movie was filmed. The "actors" were shipped in from further east in Canada. In order to make the movie more interesting, the production crew pushed

A Norway lemming is more colorful than most other lemmings. It is black and brown and has some yellow streaks. Norway lemmings live in Fennoscandia, which is a region that stretches from the Kola Peninsula in Russia west to Norway. Like other lemmings, they live under the snow in winter.

the unlucky animals off the cliff. It was not their idea to jump then or ever.[1]

There are several different kinds of lemmings including brown and collared lemmings. These two have similar behaviors and live in the same general areas in far northern Canada and Alaska. Lemmings like snow and cold, so they are right at home in the arctic regions of North America. Both kinds are mostly brown, but the collared lemming turns white in winter while the brown lemming remains brown all year.

Brown lemmings are stocky with a short muzzle and tail. They average 5.2 to 6.6 inches (13.2 to 16.8 centimeters) long with a weight of less than a quarter pound (115 grams). They are related to mice but are plumper with a much shorter tail.

A Lemming's Life on the Tundra and Taiga

Lemmings could probably win a prize for having the most babies in a year's time. The male can begin mating at four to seven weeks old while females can breed as young as two weeks old. The gestation period is only sixteen to twenty-six days long,[2] and the babies are born blind and hairless.

There are usually three to eight babies in a litter, and they grow quickly. Most have two to four litters in a year. That's a lot of lemmings. They have to reproduce quickly because they usually live a year or less in the wild.

Lemmings live on the treeless northern **tundra** and the forested **taiga** and eat plant foods. The foods they eat vary from one species to another, and can include grasses, **sedges**, mosses, forbs, roots, fruits, flowers, leaves, stems, seeds, or nuts. Brown lemmings have to eat a lot because the foods they eat are low in **nutrients**. They eat for an hour or two at a time and do this every three hours, day and night.[3]

Lemmings live in burrows in the ground, but make tunnels in the snow in winter. These tunnels help them survive the cold of arctic winters and protect them from predators.

Lemmings can be aggressive toward each other. What looks like play may be a serious wrestling match.

Lemmings may live in clumps in a common area, but they are not social animals. They are aggressive toward each other except when mating.

Many hungry animals love to catch a plump lemming for dinner. Snowy owls, arctic foxes, and wolves are a few of the species that depend on lemmings for food.

The Lemming Population Cycle

The number of lemmings naturally goes up and down in cycles. Every fourth year or so lemmings decrease in huge numbers. It takes the next three to five years for the populations to soar again before another drop-off.

Scientists think that the cycle might go something like this: One summer, the lemming population increases a lot. With so many lemmings around, predators (like snowy owls) have lots of food to eat. More baby snowy owls are born, and those baby owls have plenty of food, too. The snowy owl population increases, and more lemmings get eaten. Eventually, there aren't very many lemmings left, and so snowy owls start dying because they can't find enough food. With fewer snowy owls, more lemmings survive.

In Canada, this cycle still seems to be on track. But in Europe and Greenland, the patterns are changing.[4] It's taking lemmings longer to come back, and when they do, the increase is smaller. Scientists are still studying this problem, but many of them think that the changing climate is to blame. As the winters get warmer, there is less snow. Without the snow, lemmings can't hide from predators as easily. Species that don't normally live in the Arctic have started moving north, too. Some of these are predators that eat the lemmings. Others are rodents that eat the grasses and plants the lemmings rely on.[5]

Will Lemmings Survive?

Scientists worry that these changes could be just the beginning. If lemming numbers do not increase, there won't be enough food for any of the species that eat them. This might cause the owls and foxes to eat bird eggs instead. This could lead to fewer birds and other species in the Arctic.

Lemmings are also important because they keep the tundra grass growing and healthy by clipping the grass close to the ground. The grass grows back stronger, which helps other tundra grazers like caribou and muskoxen.

The process of a food chain is not a simple one. Many things can disturb that cycle. It is plain to see, however, that lemmings are important to the Arctic. Hopefully in the future, scientists, governments, and ordinary people can work together to make sure that lemmings don't disappear.

The Arctic Tundra

An arctic tundra biome exists in the far northern areas of the earth. Much of it is in Canada and Russia. A tundra is a treeless area where the ground remains frozen for most or all of the year. For a couple of months in the summer the average temperature is between 37 and 54 degrees Fahrenheit (3 to 12 degrees Celsius) although it can often fall below freezing. In the winter, the average temperature drops to -30 degrees Fahrenheit (-34 degrees Celsius).[6]

The arctic tundra's frozen soil layer is called permafrost. Trees cannot grow on this layer, which can be as deep as half a mile (or one kilometer). The top few inches of the soil thaw during the short summer. Then many plants and small shrubs grow quickly.

Animals like lemmings, caribou, polar bears, falcons, and salmon are able to live in the tundra **biome**. Even mosquitoes and flies live there. Some animals hibernate or migrate south during the winter because of the short supply of food.

CHAPTER NOTES

Chapter 1: Black-Tailed Prairie Dog

1. Nancy Shefferly, "*Cynomys ludovicianus*: Black-Tailed Prairie Dog," *Animal Diversity Web*, University of Michigan Museum of Zoology, 1999, http://animaldiversity.org/accounts/Cynomys_ludovicianus/

2. Russell A. Graves, *The Prairie Dog: Sentinel of the Plains* (Lubbock, TX: Texas Tech University Press, 2001), p. 11.

3. Ibid., p. 67.

4. Ibid., p. 33.

5. Shefferly, "*Cynomys ludovicianus*: Black-Tailed Prairie Dog."

6. Christie Aschwanden, "Learning to Live with the Prairie Dogs," *National Wildlife*, April-May 2001, Ebsco.

7. *National Geographic*, "Lewis and Clark Expedition Discoveries and Tribes Encountered: Plants," http://www.nationalgeographic.com/lewisandclark/resources_discoveries_plant.html; and *National Geographic*, "Lewis and Clark Expedition Discoveries and Tribes Encountered: Animals," http://www.nationalgeographic.com/lewisandclark/resources_discoveries_animal.html

8. Smithsonian National Museum of Natural History, *Lewis and Clark as Naturalists*, "Ground Rat, Burrowing Squirrel, Barking Squirrel, Petite Chien, Prairie Dog," http://www.mnh.si.edu/lewisandclark/species.cfm?id=188

Chapter 2: Bison

1. J.B. Buntjer, et al., "Phylogeny of Bovine Species Based on AFLP Fingerprinting," *Heredity*, 2002, pp. 46-51, http://www.nature.com/hdy/journal/v88/n1/full/6800007a.html

2. Linda M. Hasselstrom, *Bison: Monarch of the Plains* (Portland, OR: Graphic Arts Center Publishing, 1998), p. 93.

3. Dale Lott, *American Bison: A Natural History* (Berkeley: University of California Press, 2002) p. 76.

4. US Fish and Wildlife Service, "Time Line of the American Bison," http://www.fws.gov/bisonrange/timeline.htm

5. Judith Kohler, "6 Amazing Facts You Never Knew About Bison," *Wildlife Promise*, National Wildlife Federation, February 29, 2012, http://blog.nwf.org/2012/02/6-amazing-facts-you-never-knew-about-bison/

6. Lott, *American Bison*, pp. 5-13.

7. Ibid., p. 56.

8. Defenders of Wildlife, "Basic Facts About Bison," http://www.defenders.org/bison/basic-facts

9. Sylvia Fallon, "The Ecological Importance of Bison In Mixed-Grass Prairie Ecosystems," Buffalo Field Campaign, 2009, http://www.buffalofieldcampaign.org/habitat/documents/Fallon_The_ecological_importance_of_bison.doc

Chapter 3: Honey Bee

1. Michigan State University, "About: Pollination," Native Plants and Ecosystem Services, http://nativeplants.msu.edu/about/pollination

2. Jeff Nesbit, "Bee Colony Collapses Are More Complex Than We Thought," *US News*, August 7, 2013. http://www.usnews.com/news/blogs/at-the-edge/2013/08/07/bee-colony-collapses-are-more-complex-than-we-thought

3. Heather Pilatic, "Honey Bees—An Indicator Species in Decline," *Pesticides News*, March 2011.

CHAPTER NOTES

Chapter 4: Southern White Rhinoceros

1. San Diego Zoo Global, "White Rhinoceros, *Ceratotherium simum*," 2003, updated 2013, http://library.sandiegozoo.org/factsheets/white_rhino/white_rhino.htm

2. John R. Platt, "Only 4 Northern White Rhinos Remain in Africa: Inside the Last Attempts to Breed and Save Them," *Scientific American*, January 29, 2014, http://blogs.scientificamerican.com/extinction-countdown/2014/01/29/last-chance-northern

3. San Diego Zoo Global, "White Rhinoceros, *Ceratotherium simum*."

4. Save the Rhino International, "Poaching: The Statistics," http://www.savetherhino.org/rhino_info/poaching_statistics

5. Save The Rhino International, "White Rhino Information," http://www.savetherhino.org/rhino_info/species_of_rhino/white_rhinos/factfile_white_rhino

6. Rachel Nuwer, "Here's What Might Happen to Local Ecosystems If All the Rhinos Disappear," Smithsonian.com, February 27, 2014, http://www.smithsonianmag.com/articles/heres-what-might-happen-local-ecosystems-if-all-rhinos-disappear

7. Matthew S. Waldram, William J. Bond, and William D. Stock, "Ecological Engineering by a Mega-Grazer: White Rhino Impacts on a South African Savanna," *Ecosystems*, 2008, pp. 101-112, http://www.researchgate.net/publication/49281655_Ecological_Engineering_by_a_Mega-Grazer_White_Rhino_Impacts_on_a_South_African_Savanna/links/09e4150ae0bfe9f360000000

8. Center for Biological Diversity, "The Extinction Crisis," http://www.biologicaldiversity.org/programs/biodiversity/elements_of_biodiversity/extinction_crisis/

Chapter 5: Lemming

1. Riley Woodford, "Lemming Suicide Myth: Disney Film Faked Bogus Behavior," *Alaska Fish & Wildlife News*, September 2003, http://www.adfg.alaska.gov/index.cfm?adfg=wildlifenews.view_article&articles_id=56

2. Adrian Forsyth, *Mammals of North America: Temperate and Arctic Regions* (Buffalo, NY: Firefly Books Ltd., 1999), pp. 155-157.

3. Jennifer Barker, "*Lemmus sibiricus*, Brown Lemming," *Animal Diversity Web*, University of Michigan Museum of Zoology, 2003, http://animaldiversity.org/accounts/Lemmus_sibiricus/

4. Laura Nielsen, "Humble Lemmings Are an Arctic Keystone Species," *Frontier Scientists*, June 25, 2013, http://frontierscientists.com/2013/06/lemmings-arctic-keystone-species/

5. Lisa Gregoire, "Make Way for the Arctic's Mighty Mammal," *Nunatsiaq News*, January 21, 2011, http://www.nunatsiaqonline.ca/stories/article/98789_make_way_for_the_arctics_mighty_mammal

6. Stephanie Pullen, ed., "The Tundra Biome," *The World's Biomes*, University of California, Berkeley, April 2004, http://www.ucmp.berkeley.edu/glossary/gloss5/biome/tundra.html

WORKS CONSULTED

Aschwanden, Christie. "Learning to Live with the Prairie Dogs." *National Wildlife*, April-May 2001. Ebsco.

Barker, Jennifer. "*Lemmus sibiricus*, Brown Lemming." *Animal Diversity Web*, University of Michigan Museum of Zoology, 2003. http://animaldiversity.org/accounts/Lemmus_sibiricus/

Buntjer, J.B., M. Otsen, I.J. Nijman, M.T.R. Kuiper, and J.A. Lenstra. "Phylogeny of Bovine Species Based on AFLP Fingerprinting." *Heredity*, 2002, pp. 46-51. http://www.nature.com/hdy/journal/v88/n1/full/6800007a.html

Caro, Tim. *Conservation by Proxy: Indicator, Umbrella, Keystone, Flagship, and Other Surrogate Species*. Washington, DC: Island Press, 2010.

Center for Biological Diversity. "The Extinction Crisis." http://www.biologicaldiversity.org/programs/biodiversity/elements_of_biodiversity/extinction_crisis/

Defenders of Wildlife. "Basic Facts About Bison." http://www.defenders.org/bison/basic-facts

Eisenberg, Cristina. *The Wolf's Tooth: Keystone Predators, Trophic Cascades, and Biodiversity*. Washington, DC: Island Press, 2010.

Fallon, Sylvia. "The Ecological Importance of Bison in Mixed-Grass Prairie Ecosystems." Buffalo Field Campaign, 2009. http://www.buffalofieldcampaign.org/habitat/documents/Fallon_The_ecological_importance_of_bison.doc

Forsyth, Adrian. *Mammals of North America: Temperate and Arctic Regions*. Buffalo, NY: Firefly Books, 1999.

Fuhlendorf, Samuel D., Brady W. Allred, and Robert G. Hamilton. *Bison as Keystone Herbivores on the Great Plains*. Bronx, NY: Wildlife Conservation Society, 2010.

Graves, Russell A. *The Prairie Dog: Sentinel of the Plains*. Lubbock, TX: Texas Tech University Press, 2001.

Gregoire, Lisa. "Make Way for the Arctic's Mighty Mammal." *Nunatsiaq News*, January 21, 2011. http://www.nunatsiaqonline.ca/stories/article/98789_make_way_for_the_arctics_mighty_mammal

Hasselstrom, Linda M. *Bison: Monarch of the Plains*. Portland, OR: Graphic Arts Center Publishing, 1998.

Kohler, Judith. "6 Amazing Facts You Never Knew About Bison." *Wildlife Promise*, National Wildlife Federation, February 29, 2012. http://blog.nwf.org/2012/02/6-amazing-facts-you-never-knew-about-bison/

Lott, Dale F. *American Bison: A Natural History*. Berkeley, CA: University of California Press, 2002.

Michigan State University. "About: Pollination." Native Plants and Ecosystem Services. http://nativeplants.msu.edu/about/pollination

National Geographic. "Lewis and Clark Expedition Discoveries and Tribes Encountered: Animals." http://www.nationalgeographic.com/lewisandclark/resources_discoveries_animal.html

National Geographic. "Lewis and Clark Expedition Discoveries and Tribes Encountered: Plants." http://www.nationalgeographic.com/lewisandclark/resources_discoveries_plant.html

National Park Service. "Bison (Buffalo)—*Bison bison*." http://www.nps.gov/wica/naturescience/bison-buffalo-bison-bison.htm

Nature Conservancy. "Putting Bison Back on the Prairie." http://www.nature.org/ourinitiatives/regions/northamerica/unitedstates/northdakota/explore/putting-bison-back-on-the-prairie.xml

Nesbit, Jeff. "Bee Colony Collapses Are More Complex Than We Thought." *US News*, August 7, 2013. http://www.usnews.com/news/blogs/at-the-edge/2013/08/07/bee-colony-collapses-are-more-complex-than-we-thought

Nielsen, Laura. "Humble Lemmings Are an Arctic Keystone Species." *Frontier Scientists*, June 25, 2013. http://frontierscientists.com/2013/06/lemmings-arctic-keystone-species/

Nuwer, Rachel. "Here's What Might Happen to Local Ecosystems If All the Rhinos Disappear." Smithsonian.com, February 27, 2014. http://www.smithsonianmag.com/articles/heres-what-might-happen-local-ecosystems-if-all-rhinos-disappear

O'Toole, Christopher, and Anthony Raw. *Bees of the World*. New York: Facts On File, 1991.

Pilatic, Heather. "Honey Bees—an Indicator Species in Decline." *Pesticides News*, March 2011.

WORKS CONSULTED

Platt, John R. "Only 4 Northern White Rhinos Remain in Africa: Inside the Last Attempts to Breed and Save Them." *Scientific American*, January 29, 2014. http://blogs.scientificamerican.com/extinction-countdown/2014/01/29/last-chance-northern

Pullen, Stephanie, Editor. "The Tundra Biome." *The World's Biomes*. University of California, Berkeley, April 2004. http://www.ucmp.berkeley.edu/glossary/gloss5/biome/tundra.html

Rhino Resource Center. "Black Rhino—*Diceros bicornis*." http://www.rhinoresourcecenter.com/species/black-rhino/

Rhino Resource Center. "White Rhino—*Ceratotherium simum*." http://www.rhinoresourcecenter.com/species/white-rhino/

San Diego Zoo Global. "White Rhinoceros, *Ceratotherium simum*." 2003, updated 2013. http://library.sandiegozoo.org/factsheets/white_rhino/white_rhino.htm

Sanford, Malcolm T., and Richard E. Bonney. *Storey's Guide to Keeping Honey Bees*. North Adams, MA: Storey Publishing, 2010.

Save the Rhino International. "Poaching: The Statistics." http://www.savetherhino.org/rhino_info/poaching_statistics

Save The Rhino International. "White Rhino Information." http://www.savetherhino.org/rhino_info/species_of_rhino/white_rhinos/factfile_white_rhino

Shefferly, Nancy. "*Cynomys ludovicianus*: Black-Tailed Prairie Dog." *Animal Diversity Web*, University of Michigan Museum of Zoology, 1999. http://animaldiversity.org/accounts/Cynomys_ludovicianus/

Shivik, John. *The Predator Paradox: Ending the War with Wolves, Bears, Cougars, and Coyotes*. Boston: Beacon Press, 2014.

Smithsonian National Museum of Natural History. *Lewis and Clark as Naturalists*. "Ground Rat, Burrowing Squirrel, Barking Squirrel, Petite Chien, Prairie Dog." http://www.mnh.si.edu/lewisandclark/species.cfm?id=188

Terborgh, John, and James A. Estes, editors. *Trophic Cascades: Predators, Prey, and the Changing Dynamics of Nature*. Washington, DC: Island Press, 2010.

US Fish & Wildlife Service, South Dakota Field Office. "Black-Tailed Prairie Dog." http://fws.gov/southdakotafieldoffice/btpd.htm

US Fish and Wildlife Service. "Time Line of the American Bison." http://www.fws.gov/bisonrange/timeline.htm

Utah State Office of Education. "Buffalo Chips and Pioneers." *Life on the Trail*. Heritage Gateways. http://heritage.uen.org/resources/Wc1092520a8bc3.htm

Waldram, Matthew S., William J. Bond, and William D. Stock. "Ecological Engineering by a Mega-Grazer: White Rhino Impacts on a South African Savanna." *Ecosystems*, 2008, pp. 101-112. http://www.researchgate.net/publication/49281655_Ecological_Engineering_by_a_Mega-Grazer_White_Rhino_Impacts_on_a_South_African_Savanna/links/09e4150ae0bfe9f360000000

Woodford, Riley. "Lemming Suicide Myth: Disney Film Faked Bogus Behavior." *Alaska Fish & Wildlife News*, September 2003. http://www.adfg.alaska.gov/index.cfm?adfg=wildlifenews.view_article&articles_id=56

World Wildlife Fund. "White Rhino." https://www.worldwildlife.org/species/white-rhino

FURTHER READING

Bailer, Darice. *Prairie Dogs*. New York: Benchmark, 2012.

Becker, John E. *The North American Bison*. Farmington Hills, MI: KidHaven Press, 2003.

De Rothschild, David, editor. *Earth Matters: An Encyclopedia of Ecology*. New York: Dorling Kindersley, 2008.

Markle, Sandra. *The Case of the Vanishing Honeybees*. Minneapolis: Millbrook Press, 2014.

ON THE INTERNET

Animal Planet: Wild Animals
http://www.animalplanet.com/wild-animals

National Geographic Kids
http://kids.nationalgeographic.com

PBS Nature: American Buffalo: Spirit of a Nation
http://www.pbs.org/wnet/nature/episodes/american-buffalo-spirit-of-a-nation/introduction/2183/

PBS Nature: Bee
http://www.pbs.org/wnet/nature/category/episodes/by-animal/bee/

PBS Nature: Rhinoceros
http://www.pbs.org/wnet/nature/episodes/rhinoceros/introduction/1179/

GLOSSARY

biome (BAHY-ohm)—a community of particular kinds of plants and animals that live together in a certain region because of the climate there

conservation (kon-ser-VEY-shuhn)—saving from injury or loss

dung—manure; the waste of an animal

ecosystem (EE-koh-sis-tuhm)—a system of interaction of the plants and animals in a community

forager (FAWR-ij-er)—one who goes out and searches for food

forb (fawrb)—a broad-leaved plant that is not a grass or sedge, such as a clover or sunflower

functionally (FUHNGK-shuh-nl-ee)—practically or for the purposes of continuing on in the future

gestation (je-STEY-shuhn)—the length of time of pregnancy

immigrant (IM-i-gruhnt)—a person who moves to a new country, usually to live there permanently

larva (LAHR-vuh; plural **larvae:** LAHR-vee)—the young form of an insect that hasn't grown wings yet

litter (LIT-er)—a group of babies that an animal has at the same birth

nutrient (NOO-tree-uhnt)—substance that promotes life and good health in the body, particularly in food

ovules (OV-yools)—the plant parts that develop into seeds after fertilization

pesticide (PES-tuh-sahyd)—a chemical that is created and used for the purpose of killing pests such as insects

poacher (POH-cher)—a person who hunts an animal illegally, usually by trespassing on private or protected land

pupate (PYOO-peyt)—to change into a pupa (insect form between larva and adult) while resting, often in a cell or cocoon

range—the area that the population of a species lives in

savanna (suh-VAN-uh)—grassland areas with scattered trees, often in tropic or subtropic zones

sedge (sej)—grasslike plant with a solid triangular stem that usually lives near water

suicide (SOO-uh-sahyd)—the act of killing oneself on purpose

taiga (TAHY-guh)—a biome that exists in northern North America, Europe, and Asia, which has forests with large numbers of pine, spruce, and larch trees

trophy hunting (TROH-fee HUHN-ting)—killing an animal for something other than food, sometimes for a head or other body part to keep as a souvenir

tundra (TUHN-druh)—the flat, treeless plain biome that exists in the arctic areas of North America, Europe, and Asia

INDEX

INDEX

About the Author

Bonnie Hinman has loved studying nature since she was a child growing up on her family's farm. Today she is a certified Missouri Master Naturalist and works in her community educating children and adults about the natural world around them. She also volunteers her time to restore and maintain the local ecosystem. Hinman has had more than thirty books published including Mitchell Lane's *Threat to the Leatherback Turtle*. She lives with her husband Bill in Joplin, Missouri, near her children and five grandchildren.